Expert AI Models

Transforming Industries with Tailored AI Solutions

Taylor Royce

DEDICATION

To everyone who has the guts to inquire, investigate, and create. The pioneers who think beyond the norm and dare to influence the future with audacious ideas and unwavering resolve are honored in this book.

To those of you who dream, think, and do—may your curiosity never be satisfied and may your efforts always motivate those who come after you.

For their constant encouragement, support, and faith in me during this journey, I also dedicate this work to my family and friends. I have always found strength in your love and understanding.

Last but not least, I hope this book will serve as a small flame to kindle your passion for the possibilities of the future and encourage you to set out on your own path of discovery.

DISCLAIMER

This book contains information that should only be used for general informative purposes. Although every attempt has been made to guarantee the content's accuracy and dependability, the author and publisher make no guarantees or representations about the information's completeness, accuracy, or applicability.

Before making decisions based on the information in this book, readers should obtain appropriate consultation from qualified experts as this book is not meant to be a source of professional advice. Any liabilities, losses, or damages resulting from the use or reliance on any information in this book are not the responsibility of the author or publisher.

Additionally, the scenarios, case studies, and examples offered are merely instances and might not accurately represent the unique situation of any given person or business. All product names, company names, and trademarks included in this book belong to their respective owners and are only used for identification.

As new advancements in AI and technology continue to be made, the information in this book may change. By consulting other sources and keeping abreast of current trends and best practices, the author urges readers to stay informed.

CONTENTS

ACKNOWLEDGMENTS...1

CHAPTER 1...1

An Overview of AI Expert Models...1

1.1 The Development of Artificial Intelligence: From General to Expert Models...1

1.2 The definition of expert models...3

1.3 Customization's Contribution to AI Maturity........................5

CHAPTER 2...10

Expert Models' Business Case...10

2.1 Using Tailored AI to Drive Exponential Value....................10

2.2 Custom AI Models' Competitive Advantages.......................12

2.3 Expert Model Development Cost-Benefit Analysis...............15

CHAPTER 3...20

Expert Model Adoption in Key Industries.................................20

3.1 Healthcare: Diagnostics and Precision Medicine.................20

3.2 Finance: Risk Management and Fraud Detection..................22

3.3 Manufacturing: Quality Control and Predictive Maintenance........25

CHAPTER 4...29

IT Maturity's Impact on AI Adoption..29

4.1 Knowing the Levels of IT Maturity.....................................29

4.2 Transformers in Comparison to Ordinary IT Departments............31

4.3 Case Studies: Leading AI Adoption by High-Maturity Firms........34

CHAPTER 5...38

Expert Model Design and Development......................................38

5.1 Working Together with Subject Matter Experts.............................. 38

5.2 Expert Model Data Collection and Preprocessing......................... 40

5.3 Making Use of Cutting-Edge Methods: Transfer Learning and

Fine-Tuning...43

CHAPTER 6..46

The difficulties in creating and implementing expert models are

covered...46

6.1 Data Difficulties: Privacy, Access, and Bias.................................46

6.2 Integration and Technical Barriers...48

6.3 Developmental Skill and Cost Gaps... 50

CHAPTER 7..54

Assessing and Tracking Expert Model Performance............................. 54

7.1 Specifying AI Model Success Metrics...54

7.2 Expert Model Maintenance and Monitoring..................................58

7.3 Feedback Loops for Ongoing Improvement.................................. 60

CHAPTER 8..65

Expert Models' Future.. 65

8.1 Expert Models Shaped by Emerging Technologies....................... 65

8.2 The Combination of Generative AI and Expert Models................ 70

8.3 Expert Model Scenarios for 2030 and Later..................................74

CHAPTER 9..79

Regulatory and Ethical Aspects.. 79

9.1 Making Sure Expert Models Are Fair and Open........................... 80

9.2 Managing Industry Standards and Regulations............................. 85

9.3 Establishing Credibility with AI Systems.....................................88

CHAPTER 10..93

Expert Model Adoption Strategies for Organizations........................... 93

10.1 Evaluating AI Implementation Readiness.................................... 93

10.2 Creating an AI Roadmap: From Idea to Implementation............. 99

10.3 Working with Partners and AI Vendors...................................... 104

ABOUT THE AUTHOR..109

ACKNOWLEDGMENTS

From the bottom of my heart, I want to thank everyone who helped make this book possible. This project would not have been possible without your help, direction, and inspiration.

I want to start by expressing my gratitude to my family and friends for their unwavering support and faith in me. Throughout this journey, your steadfast support has been my compass, and I sincerely appreciate your understanding and patience.

A particular thank you is extended to the professionals and specialists in the fields of technology and artificial intelligence, whose skills and insights have substantially impacted the content of this book. Your input has enhanced the concepts discussed here, whether it has been from formal conversations, research, or the sharing of personal experiences.

I am especially appreciative to my mentors and coworkers, who provided insightful criticism and direction as this work was being developed. Your knowledge has contributed to making this book a more thorough and perceptive guide.

We appreciate your time and interest in this work, readers. I hope the information presented here encourages you to research, develop, and add to the rapidly expanding subject of artificial intelligence.

Finally, I want to thank all of the people who have contributed behind the scenes, including publishers, editors, and designers. Your expertise and commitment to excellence have been crucial in making this book a reality.

I genuinely appreciate each and every one of you, and this work is a reflection of our combined enthusiasm and effort.

CHAPTER 1

AN OVERVIEW OF AI EXPERT MODELS

1.1 The Development of Artificial Intelligence: From General to Expert Models

Over the past few decades, artificial intelligence (AI) has undergone significant change. The main objective of early AI systems was to serve as all-purpose instruments that could handle general tasks like speech processing, language translation, and image recognition. Despite the fact that these methods have been revolutionary, their shortcomings are revealed when dealing with the complex issues of particular sectors.

While general artificial intelligence models are excellent at managing large datasets and carrying out general tasks, they frequently lack the accuracy needed for highly specialized applications. For example:

When it comes to producing industry-specific outputs, like

writing a legal document or making medical diagnosis, a broad language model may perform admirably when it comes to text generation. Similar to this, image recognition algorithms that were trained on generic datasets might not perform well in specific applications, such as finding manufacturing flaws or recognizing irregularities in medical imaging.

The inability of universal models to handle domain-specific complications is the source of their limits. Without considerable refinement, generic AI is unable to provide the accuracy, context awareness, and adaptability that many industries demand. This deficiency opened the door for expert models, AI systems that are carefully crafted to meet the particular needs of particular sectors.

The following are some of the main forces behind this shift:

- **Demand for Higher Accuracy**: Because sectors like healthcare and finance cannot afford mistakes, they require AI systems that adhere to strict accuracy requirements.
- **Regulatory Compliance:** Customized solutions are

required because general AI models are frequently ill-prepared to handle industry-specific laws.

- **Operational Efficiency:** By eliminating the need to modify generic solutions to suit industrial demands, customized AI increases productivity and lowers expenses.

Given this, expert models offer a new degree of complexity and applicability, making them the natural next stage in the growth of AI.

1.2 The definition of expert models

Expert models are AI programs created and honed to handle the unique opportunities, demands, and difficulties of a given sector or field. These models are designed to interpret domain-specific data and produce results that are not as accurate or pertinent as those produced by broad AI models.

Features of Expert Models:

- **Domain Specialization:** In contrast to general AI, expert models are specifically designed for sectors like manufacturing, logistics, healthcare, and finance. An expert model for healthcare, for example, might focus on diagnosing illnesses via diagnostic photos or evaluating electronic medical information.

- The accuracy is high. Expert models outperform general models in terms of precision by concentrating on a particular topic.

- **Contextualization of Data:** Expert models are skilled at comprehending context and subtleties that generic AI can miss since they integrate domain-specific knowledge.

Purpose and Benefits:

- **Solving Unique Industry Problems:** Expert models tackle issues that general AI finds difficult, such real-time decision-making in autonomous cars or regulatory compliance in banking.

- **Improving Decision-Making:** These models enable firms to make data-driven decisions with greater assurance by utilizing domain-specific insights.

- **Improving Operational Efficiency:** Tailored AI solutions automate operations with unmatched accuracy, streamlining procedures.

The following are some instances of expert models in action:

1. **Healthcare:** AI-powered diagnostic systems that use medical imaging to identify diseases like cancer.
2. **Finance:** Fraud detection systems that look for anomalous patterns unique to banking by analyzing transactional data.
3. **Retail:** Tools for customer analytics that forecast consumer behavior and enhance inventory control.

In conclusion, expert models are produced by fusing sophisticated AI capabilities with in-depth domain knowledge, resulting in intelligent and contextually aware systems.

1.3 Customization's Contribution to AI Maturity

A key component of reaching high AI maturity in enterprises is customizing AI models. The ability of a company to create, implement, and use AI for both strategic and operational advantages is referred to as AI maturity.

How AI Maturity Is Improved by Customization:

1. Improved Adoption Rates:

- Because tailored AI solutions directly target certain problem spots, they are more popular with stakeholders across sectors.
- For instance, logistics firms are more likely to use an AI tool made specifically for supply chain optimization than a general optimization algorithm.

2. More Accuracy and Relevance:

- Industry-specific data is used in custom models to guarantee that predictions and insights are precise and useful.
- Expert models can identify subtle flaws that generic AI systems could overlook in industries like manufacturing, guaranteeing greater quality standards.

3. Alignment with Business Goals:

- Expert models provide more significant results when

they are in line with an organization's strategic objectives.

- For example, a financial company can adapt its AI for fraud detection to fit organizational risk tolerance and local compliance regulations.

Affecting IT Departments:

"Transformers," or organizations with a high level of AI maturity, are adept at incorporating expert models into their processes. Information technology reports state:

- By 2025, 80% of IT departments with high maturity have either invested in or intend to implement AI solutions.
- Compared to their less developed peers, these departments are twice as likely to see exponential value from AI.

Transformers and Expert Models:

- **Proactive Approach:** High-maturity companies take a proactive stance by making early investments in specialized AI solutions.
- **Resource Allocation:** These companies set aside

enough funds for the development and upkeep of expert models, including infrastructure and qualified staff.

- Transformers provide continued relevance and performance by iteratively updating and optimizing their models in response to feedback and new data.

Advantages for Businesses:

- **Operational Excellence:** Tailored AI promotes productivity by resolving process-specific obstacles.
- **Regulatory Compliance:** Expert models lower the risk of non-compliance by making it easier to follow industry regulations.
- One of the strategic advantages is Businesses that use customized AI models are more likely to surpass rivals and gain market share.

Difficulties of Customization:

- **Resource Intensive:** Developing expert models necessitates a large time, talent, and infrastructure investment.
- **Data Dependency:** The quality and accessibility of domain-specific data are critical to the efficacy of

tailored models.

- **Requirements for Maintenance:** As industries change, expert models need to be updated frequently to stay current.

Expert models are essential for businesses looking to reach high AI maturity because, in spite of these difficulties, the advantages of customization greatly exceed the disadvantages.

An overview of expert models, their development, and their function in promoting organizational performance is given in this chapter. Businesses can uncover unmatched value and obtain a competitive edge in their respective industries by switching from general to expert AI systems.

CHAPTER 2

EXPERT MODELS' BUSINESS CASE

2.1 Using Tailored AI to Drive Exponential Value

Artificial intelligence (AI) is a major factor in the remarkable pace at which the business landscape is changing. Expert models, one of AI's numerous developments, have become effective instruments for generating exponential value by providing companies with accuracy, effectiveness, and useful insights that generic AI models frequently fall short of.

Exponential Returns Unlocked

Expert models are made to handle the particular opportunities and difficulties faced by particular sectors. Businesses can do the following by customizing AI solutions to match their objectives:

- **Enhanced Ability to Make Decisions:** Accurate and contextually relevant insights are offered by custom models. For instance, by examining seasonality, buying patterns, and regional preferences, a retail business using an expert AI model can more accurately forecast customer trends.

- **Efficiency in Operations:** Internal processes are optimized using expert models, which lower expenses and boost output. For example, predictive maintenance models in manufacturing detect equipment breakdowns before they happen, preventing expensive downtime.

- **Improved Risk Management:** Tailored AI systems that can more accurately identify anomalies or possible hazards are extremely beneficial to sectors like healthcare and finance.

An example of this might be:

An expert model was used by a logistics company to optimize delivery routes by taking weather, traffic patterns, and fuel efficiency into consideration. The outcome showed the cumulative benefits of customized AI systems, resulting in a 20% reduction in delivery times and a notable drop in operating expenses.

The following are the primary advantages:

1. **Precision and precision:** Expert models that are focused on domain-specific data provide predictions and analyses with unmatched precision.

2. **greater Adoption Rates:** Customized solutions are more well-liked by stakeholders, which makes implementation easier and usage greater.

3. **Scalability:** After being put into practice, expert models can be expanded to accommodate bigger datasets and more diverse applications, thereby increasing their influence.

By using expert models, businesses are laying the groundwork for exponential development rather than just enhancing their present operations.

2.2 Custom AI Models' Competitive Advantages

Standing out in today's fiercely competitive marketplaces frequently calls for accuracy in addition to creativity. Expert models give companies a significant advantage by facilitating quick, accurate, and flexible operations.

1. Faster Product Development:

- By integrating expert AI systems into research and development, businesses may expedite the design, testing, and iteration of products. This is one way that businesses use expert models to gain an advantage.

- For instance, pharmaceutical companies shorten development times from years to months by using customized AI models to find new drug prospects.

2. Enhanced Customer Experiences:

- Businesses may provide their clients with individualized experiences by utilizing unique AI solutions.

- In order to increase conversion rates and consumer pleasure, retail behemoths employ expert models to suggest products based on browsing history, purchase trends, and even mood indications.

3. Operational Excellence:

- Expert models assist companies in achieving operational excellence by automating repetitive processes, optimizing resource allocation, and streamlining supply chains. One prominent example is the application of AI in the automobile sector, where robots on assembly lines are guided by expert models to complete tasks with the fewest possible faults, thus lowering production costs.

Practical Illustrations of Competitive Advantage:

- **Healthcare:** A top hospital network used an expert model to forecast patient admission rates, which allowed for more efficient use of resources and shorter wait times.

- **Finance**: A multinational bank reduced fraud-related losses by 40% in the first year after implementing a fraud detection system customized to its transaction patterns.

- **E-commerce:** By using an expert model to optimize inventory management, an online shop was able to increase customer happiness and sales by guaranteeing that high-demand products were always available.

Important Takeaway:

Businesses that use expert models not only meet but

frequently exceed industry standards, establishing themselves as leaders in their domains.

2.3 Expert Model Development Cost-Benefit Analysis

The costs and possible returns of investing in expert models must be carefully considered. Expert models need time, money, and specialized knowledge, in contrast to off-the-shelf AI systems, which are less expensive and easier to implement. But frequently, the long-term advantages outweigh the initial outlay.

Comprehending the Expenses:

1. Development Costs:
- Hiring domain experts, data scientists, and engineers is one of the major up-front expenses involved in creating an expert model.
- Organizations also need to make investments in computational infrastructure for model training, as well as in high-quality data collecting and annotation.

2. Maintenance and Updates:

- Expert models need to be updated frequently to stay current and useful, particularly in dynamic industries where laws and trends change quickly.

3. Implementation Costs:

- Additional resources are required for the critical steps of staff training, system integration, and business process alignment.

1. The benefits are calculated as follows:

- **Higher ROI:** Domain-specific insights from expert models lead to improved operational efficiency and decision-making, which in turn boost profitability. By decreasing overstock and understock problems, for instance, a store who spends $500,000 on a demand forecasting model may recoup this expense in less than a year.

2. Decreased Operational Costs:

- Expert model-enabled automation reduces manual intervention, which lowers labor expenses and mistake rates.

- By preventing unscheduled downtime, manufacturing facilities that use AI for predictive maintenance save millions of dollars every year.

3. Strategic Advantage:

- Businesses can gain a competitive edge that frequently results in market leadership by anticipating trends, optimizing resources, and customizing offers.

Framework for ROI Analysis:

Companies can take the following actions to determine if creating an expert model is beneficial:

- **Identify Key Metrics**: Establish what constitutes success. Metrics could include, for example, revenue growth, cost savings, or error reduction.
- **Estimate Costs:** Take into consideration the costs of development, implementation, and upkeep.
- **Project Benefits**: To calculate the possible benefits of implementing the concept, use case studies, pilot programs, or simulations.
- **Conduct a Break-Even Analysis**: Determine the time it will take for the advantages to outweigh the

initial expenses.

A Comparative Analysis of Off-the-Shelf Solutions

In the short term, general AI models could seem more affordable, but they frequently lack the accuracy and applicability needed for intricate industry-specific problems. Despite being more costly, expert models offer:

- **Personalized Solutions:** Comply flawlessly with corporate objectives.

- Long-term flexibility and growth potential are provided by scalability and adaptability.

Details:

The value proposition of creating expert models is amply demonstrated by the cost-benefit analysis. The benefits of investing in these customized solutions for businesses include continuous development, competitive advantages, and exponential returns.

This chapter emphasizes the need of expert models for businesses hoping to prosper in a cutthroat, data-driven environment. Expert models are a key component of contemporary AI strategy since they generate exponential value, provide for competitive advantages, and provide measurable benefits to offset their expenses.

CHAPTER 3

Expert Model Adoption in Key Industries

3.1 Healthcare: Diagnostics and Precision Medicine

By utilizing AI's ability to revolutionize patient care and medical procedures, the healthcare industry has led the way in implementing expert models. Healthcare practitioners are tackling difficult problems, increasing diagnostic precision, and customizing treatment regimens by employing customized AI solutions.

Diagnostics Transformation

Through their ability to spot patterns in medical data that are too delicate for human inspection, expert models are revolutionizing the diagnostics industry. With unparalleled accuracy, these algorithms examine genetic sequences, imaging data, and patient histories.

- **Radiology:** AI-powered tools help radiologists find abnormalities in X-rays, MRIs, and CT scans, such as tumors, fractures, or lesions. An expert model trained on thousands of mammograms, for example, is more accurate than conventional techniques at detecting breast cancer in its early stages.

- **Pathology:** AI models examine biopsy slides and tissue samples to detect abnormal cell structures, facilitating faster and more precise diagnosis.

Precision Medicine

The foundation of contemporary medicine is individualized treatment, and the realization of precision medicine depends heavily on expert models.

- **Genomics:** Customized AI models examine a patient's genetic composition to detect illness susceptibilities and suggest tailored therapies or preventative actions.
- **Management of Chronic Disease:** Expert models track patient data in real-time for diseases like diabetes or hypertension, anticipating problems and delivering prompt treatments.

Sped-up Drug Discovery

The time and expense involved in creating new

medications are greatly decreased by using expert models. These models forecast which chemicals are most likely to be successful in clinical trials by examining molecular interactions.

- AI systems, for instance, have found possible cures for rare diseases in months as opposed to years in the past.

Better Results for Patients

- Improved diagnostic accuracy is one way that the use of expert models in healthcare guarantees improved patient outcomes.
- Offering treatment plans based on data.
- Reducing misdiagnosis and medical blunders.

3.2 Finance: Risk Management and Fraud Detection

Another important user of expert models is the finance industry, which uses AI to evaluate risks, fight fraud, and expedite compliance procedures. The requirement for accurate and flexible AI solutions is critical as financial transactions become more digital.

Quick and Accurate Fraud Detection

Because financial fraud is always changing, organizations must maintain a competitive edge by implementing strong detection systems.

- **Real-Time Monitoring:** To spot suspect activity, such odd spending patterns or unauthorized access, expert models examine transactional data in real-time.

- **Behavioral Analysis:** AI systems monitor user behavior to identify deviations and set baselines. For instance, the system can notify authorities if a credit card is unexpectedly used in several places in a matter of minutes.

Risk Management and Assessment

Financial organizations can make better judgments by using expert models to assess risks more precisely.

- **Credit Scoring:** To forecast loan repayment capacities, AI models examine job information, credit histories, and spending trends.

- **Portfolio Administration:** Expert models offer investment advice that are customized to meet the objectives of individuals or institutions by examining market movements and economic factors.

Improving Compliance Procedures

For financial institutions, maintaining regulatory compliance is a crucial yet resource-intensive undertaking. These procedures are automated and made simpler using expert models.

- **Document Analysis:** To ensure compliance with legal requirements, AI systems examine vast amounts of contracts, reports, and regulatory guidelines.

- Anomaly Detection: Tailored models identify possible violations of compliance, lowering the possibility of fines.

Practical Uses in Finance

- An international bank used an expert model to track high-frequency trading activity, spotting fraudulent trends and averting losses.

- AI is used by insurance firms to evaluate claims, identify fraudulent submissions and accelerate valid ones.

- By using expert models, the financial sector not only

protects assets but also increases client trust by improving security and transparency.

3.3 Manufacturing: Quality Control and Predictive Maintenance

Expert model integration has transformed operations in manufacturing by streamlining procedures, reducing downtime, and guaranteeing constant product quality.

The use of predictive maintenance

Predictive maintenance, which moves the emphasis from reactive to proactive equipment management, is one of the most significant applications of expert models in manufacturing.

- **Analyzing Sensor Data:** AI models keep an eye on machine sensors to identify temperature, vibration, or pressure anomalies, potentially averting breakdowns before they happen.
- **Reducing Downtime:** Manufacturers can prevent expensive disruptions by planning maintenance for scheduled downtimes.
- Expert AI systems, for instance, helped a car

assembly facility save millions of dollars a year by reducing machine downtime by 30%.

Improving Quality Control

By detecting flaws instantly, expert models guarantee that goods fulfill strict quality requirements.

- **Visual Inspection:** AI-powered cameras are able to identify little flaws in parts that human inspectors would miss.

- **Process Optimization:** Expert models analyze production data and suggest changes to ensure consistent quality.

Simplifying Supply Chains

AI models are essential for supply chain management because they guarantee the timely delivery of both raw materials and completed goods.

- **Demand Forecasting:** Manufacturers can prevent overproduction or stock outs by using expert models that forecast market demand with high precision.

- **Management of Inventory:** AI systems optimize inventory levels by examining market trends and historical data, which lowers waste and storage expenses.

Practices for Sustainable Manufacturing

- Expert models also optimize energy use, which promotes sustainability.
- Minimizing the waste of materials.
- Through accurate material sorting, recycling and reusability are made possible.

Actual Manufacturing Success Stories

- A consumer electronics manufacturer reduced defect rates by 25% by implementing AI-driven quality control tools.
- Predictive maintenance was employed by an aerospace manufacturer to increase the dependability of vital equipment, resulting in safer operations and financial savings.

By tackling their particular problems and optimizing operational effectiveness, expert models are transforming industries. They offer accuracy in diagnosis and therapy in the medical field. They improve decision-making and strengthen security in the financial industry. They promote sustainability and efficiency in manufacturing. The revolutionary influence of expert models keeps growing as more industries embrace these customized AI solutions, opening the door to a more intelligent and effective future.

CHAPTER 4

IT Maturity's Impact on AI Adoption

4.1 Knowing the Levels of IT Maturity

The term "IT maturity" describes how an organization's IT capabilities, procedures, and tactics change over time. An organization's capacity to embrace, implement, and reap the benefits of cutting-edge technology like expert AI models is largely determined by its IT maturity levels.

Identifying the Levels of IT Maturity

An organization's technological expertise and alignment with business objectives are reflected in the phases of IT maturity. These phases consist of:

- At this early stage, IT operations are largely reactive and poorly aligned with business objectives. AI investments are either infrequent or badly handled.

- **Developing Stage**: Although there is some integration of technology into company operations and more structured IT processes, there is little innovation.

- **Optimized Stage:** With cutting-edge capabilities like AI incorporated into operations and decision-making, IT is a key enabler of business strategies.

Higher IT maturity organizations are better able to spot opportunities, use expert AI models efficiently, and adjust to changing market demands.

Impact on AI Adoption

- **Innovation Capability:** IT departments with high maturity have the infrastructure, expertise, and mentality necessary to test and deploy AI technologies.
- **Strategic Alignment:** To ensure relevance and effect, these firms match AI initiatives with long-term business objectives.
- The effective allocation of resources by mature IT teams guarantees sufficient funds, personnel, and assistance for AI projects.

Developing IT Maturity

- Enhancing IT governance and leadership is a key priority for organizations looking to increase their IT maturity.
- Making investments in skill-building and talent development.
- Adopting a mindset that values ongoing innovation and development.

4.2 Transformers in Comparison to Ordinary IT Departments

The difference between normal and high-maturity IT departments often referred to as "Transformers" is substantial. The degree of success in using expert models for business transformation is determined by this gap, which also affects the adoption of AI.

The attributes of transformers

Transformers have unique characteristics that distinguish them:

- **Proactive Approach:** They invest in cutting-edge technologies like artificial intelligence (AI) ahead of their rivals because they predict technological trends.

- These departments prioritize data collection, analysis, and integration across all functions, exhibiting a data-driven culture.

- IT teams collaborate closely with business departments to ensure that AI models are able to tackle real-world problems. This is known as cross-functional collaboration.

- **Sturdy Infrastructure:** Cloud platforms, sophisticated IT systems, and safe data pipelines facilitate the smooth implementation of AI.

Methods Used by Transformers

- **Custom AI Development:** Transformers frequently place a high priority on creating expert models that are specific to their requirements, guaranteeing optimal efficacy and relevance.

- **Scalable Solutions:** They create AI solutions that can grow with the company and change to meet evolving needs.

- **Ongoing Education**: By funding training initiatives, these companies make sure staff members are knowledgeable on the most recent developments in artificial intelligence.

Results Achieved by Transformers

- **Exponential Value:** Compared to typical IT departments, Transformers have double the chance of generating exponential returns on AI investments.

- **Market Leadership:** By innovating more quickly and providing better client experiences, these companies get a competitive advantage.

- **Operational Efficiency:** Predictive analytics and process automation boost output while cutting expenses.

Difficulties Average IT Departments Face

- **Limited Vision:** These departments find it difficult to defend investments in expert models in the absence of a clear AI strategy.

- **Skill Gaps:** Adoption and deployment of AI are hampered by a lack of technical knowledge.

- **Infrastructure Constraints:** The potential of AI solutions is limited by outdated systems and data silos.

Organizations can pinpoint areas for development and map out a course for greater IT maturity by examining the differences between Transformers and typical IT departments.

4.3 Case Studies: Leading AI Adoption by High-Maturity Firms

Examples from the real world offer insightful information about how high-maturity IT departments use expert models to produce game-changing results.

Case Study 1: AI-Powered Precision Agriculture

- **Company:** An international agribusiness company.
- Unpredictable weather and soil conditions cause inconsistent agricultural yields, which is a challenge.
- **Remedy:** To give farmers exact planting, irrigation, and fertilization suggestions, the company created an expert AI model that examined soil data, satellite photos, and weather forecasts.

Result:
- Crop yields increased by 20%.
- Reduced use of fertilizer and water, improving

sustainability.

- Farmers' decision-making is improved, increasing their profitability.

Key Takeaways:

- Advanced analytics and data integration were utilized by high-maturity IT teams.
- The applicability of AI models to the agriculture sector was guaranteed through customization.

Case Study 2: Scalable Retail Personalization

- The company is a well-known online shop.
- Low customer engagement and high cart abandonment rates provide a challenge.
- **Solution:** To provide dynamic pricing and personalized product recommendations, the retailer deployed an expert AI model that examined consumer browsing patterns, past purchases, and behavior.

Result:

- The sales conversion rate increased by 35%.
- Increased client loyalty and pleasure.
- Effective demand forecasting for inventory

management.

Key Takeaways:

- The smooth integration of AI into customer-facing procedures was made possible by a data-driven culture.

- The marketing and IT departments worked together to guarantee alignment with corporate objectives.

Case Study 3: Manufacturing Predictive Maintenance

The company in question is a multinational automaker.

- Frequent equipment failures that result in production delays and higher expenses provide a challenge.

- **Solution:** To track machine performance, identify irregularities, and anticipate possible failures, the manufacturer implemented an expert AI model.

Result:

- A 30% decrease in unscheduled downtime.

- Reduce maintenance expenses by implementing focused solutions.

- Improved uniformity and quality of the product.

Key Takeaways:

- Real-time data processing was backed by advanced IT infrastructure.

- Proactive decision-making was facilitated by AI-driven insights.

IT maturity is a fundamental enabler that organizations must prioritize if they want to fully utilize expert models. Businesses may establish themselves as leaders in AI adoption by analyzing their maturity levels, taking inspiration from Transformers, and looking at successful case studies. Investments in technology are necessary for this journey, but so is a dedication to encouraging creativity, teamwork, and ongoing development.

CHAPTER 5

EXPERT MODEL DESIGN AND DEVELOPMENT

Expert AI model development is a complex process that calls for a well-balanced combination of technical know-how and sector-specific understanding. In order to ensure that expert models satisfy the particular requirements of the sectors they are meant for, this chapter delves deeply into the fundamentals of their design and development.

5.1 Working Together with Subject Matter Experts

When it comes to creating expert AI models, domain expertise is essential. These people ensure that AI solutions are not only technically sound but also practically applicable by contributing their extensive knowledge and contextual understanding of particular sectors.

The Importance of Industry Experience

AI engineers frequently have strong programming and algorithm design skills, but they might not have in-depth knowledge of particular industries, such as manufacturing, healthcare, or finance. Domain specialists fill this void by offering:

- **Insights into Industry-Specific Challenges:** They pinpoint opportunities and problems that are exclusive to their industry.

- **Model Output Validation:** Professionals make sure AI-generated outcomes meet industry standards and real-world expectations.

- **Recommendations for Rules and Adherence**: Finance and healthcare are two highly regulated industries. Domain specialists ensure AI models follow moral and legal requirements.

Tips for Successful Cooperation

- **Cross-Functional Teams:** To guarantee a range of viewpoints, put together teams of AI developers, subject matter experts, and business strategists.

- **Workshops and Knowledge-Sharing Sessions**: Encourage frequent dialogues to match domain-specific and technical objectives.

- **Loops of Iterative Feedback:** To improve accuracy and relevance, domain experts should periodically examine and improve the model's results.

An example from the real world

AI diagnostic models frequently work with medical professionals in the healthcare industry to understand difficult data, such as radiology pictures. Errors could result from the AI misinterpreting anomalies if a radiologist isn't involved.

5.2 Expert Model Data Collection and Preprocessing

The quality of the data used to train an AI model is its cornerstone. Expert models, which are tailored to particular sectors, need datasets that capture the distinctive features of their field.

The Value of Industry-Specific Information

- The complexities of specialized industries are sometimes missed by general databases. For instance, soil composition information and satellite photos are essential for precision farming models in the agricultural industry.

- Fraud detection systems in the financial industry require market trends and transaction histories.

Data Acquisition Methods

- **Internal Data Sources**: Make use of organizational data like operations logs, customer records, or past performance measurements.

- **Publicly Available Datasets:** Make use of publicly accessible datasets that are pertinent to the sector. Take genomic datasets for medical purposes, for example.

- **Third-Party Providers:** Collaborate with data suppliers who focus on selecting data sets unique to a given industry.

- **Real-Time Data Collection:** Use sensors or Internet of Things devices to collect data in real-time, especially in manufacturing and other industries.

Techniques for Preprocessing Data

Model performance may be harmed by the noise and inconsistencies that are frequently present in raw data. Preprocessing guarantees the quality of the data by:

- Eliminating outliers, filling in missing numbers, and removing duplicates are all examples of data cleaning.

- Standardizing data formats to guarantee consistency across datasets is known as "normalization and scaling."

- Accurate labeling and annotation are essential for supervised learning. This is particularly important in fields like medical imaging.

- Finding the most pertinent variables to increase the accuracy and efficiency of the model is known as "feature selection."

Difficulties and Solutions

- **Difficulty:** In specialist businesses, access to high-quality data is limited.

- **Solution:** Add synthetic data production to real-world datasets.

- Data bias that produces skewed results is the challenge. The solution is to use fairness audits and a variety of data sampling methods.

5.3 Making Use of Cutting-Edge Methods: Transfer Learning and Fine-Tuning

Building expert models from the ground up might take a lot of effort and resources. Methods such as fine-tuning and transfer learning greatly speed up this process without sacrificing performance.

A Comprehensive Overview of Transfer Learning

Using a previously trained model as a foundation for creating a new model is known as transfer learning. These pre-trained models, which are frequently created using sizable generic datasets, offer a strong basis by providing:

- **Pre-Learned Features:** The model is already aware of fundamental patterns, such text sentiment or image borders.
- **Decreased Training Duration:** Less time and computing resources are needed because the model already contains information.

Transfer Learning in Expert Models

- **Healthcare:** Targeting medical imaging tasks like tumor detection with pre-trained image recognition models like ResNet.

- **Finance:** Using models for natural language processing, such as BERT, to analyze financial reports and documents.

Customization through Fine-Tuning

Fine-tuning is the process of honing a previously trained model to focus on a particular job or domain. This includes:

- Retraining the last layers involves modifying the neural network's top layers to concentrate on characteristics unique to a given business.
- **Adding Domain-Specific Data:** Adding specific industry data to the initial training dataset.
- **Optimizing Hyperparameters**: Modifying factors like batch sizes and learning rates to improve model performance.

Advantages of Transfer Learning and Fine-Tuning

- **Cost-Effective:** Businesses save money on infrastructure and computational resources.
- **Higher Accuracy:** Using previously learned information frequently yields better performance

than models created from the ground up.

- The time-to-market for AI solutions can be accelerated by the quicker operationalization of models.

Transfer Learning in Action as an Example

An AI-powered legal assistant is created by fine-tuning a pre-trained natural language processing model, such as GPT, using legal texts. The assistant is very skilled in contract drafting, case law analysis, and identifying discrepancies in legal papers.

Expert model design and development is a challenging but worthwhile process that calls for teamwork, careful data handling, and the calculated application of cutting-edge methods. Organizations may develop AI solutions that are accurate, effective, and highly relevant to their businesses by combining domain expertise, guaranteeing data quality, and utilizing transfer learning. These procedures serve as the cornerstone of an expert AI model's successful development, giving companies access to unmatched operational value.

CHAPTER 6

THE DIFFICULTIES IN CREATING AND IMPLEMENTING EXPERT MODELS ARE COVERED

Although the creation and application of expert AI models has the potential to revolutionize many industries, there are drawbacks. Navigating these challenges successfully necessitates a sophisticated grasp of the challenges that companies encounter, ranging from resource limitations and technical difficulties to data complexities. This chapter presents a thorough examination of these difficulties along with suggestions for successfully overcoming them.

6.1 Data Difficulties: Privacy, Access, and Bias

Expert AI models rely heavily on data, yet managing and acquiring it presents fundamental difficulties.

Access to Quality Data
- **Limited Availability in Specialized Domains:**

Accurate model training may be challenging in some areas, such as specialist manufacturing or uncommon illness research, which may lack strong datasets.

- **Fragmented Data Sources:** Data may be spread across several silos, necessitating laborious and resource-intensive integration processes.

- **Dynamic Data Needs:** To keep models relevant, industries like retail and finance need real-time data, which presents additional logistical issues.

Assuring Compliance with Privacy

Ensuring data privacy has become a crucial problem due to the proliferation of international regulations like the CCPA, GDPR, and HIPAA:

- **Sensitive Data Handling**: Highly confidential data is handled by the healthcare, financial, and other sectors. If you handle it poorly, you risk losing people's trust and facing legal consequences.

- Strong anonymization and pseudonymization techniques must be used, although they are frequently difficult and resource-intensive to implement.

- **Consent Management**: Companies need to make sure that the right procedures are in place to get and handle user consent for the use of their data.

Reducing Data Bias

The fairness and dependability of expert models can be diminished by bias in training data, which can provide skewed outputs:

- **The types of bias include:** These include algorithmic bias (unintended consequences of model design), historical bias (reinforcement of out-of-date trends), and sampling bias (underrepresentation of particular populations).

Mitigation Strategies:

- Perform fairness checks while developing the model.
- Make use of representative and varied datasets.
- Use adversarial debiasing strategies to identify and address bias instantly.

6.2 Integration and Technical Barriers

Expert models have a complicated technical environment, and incorporating them into current systems frequently presents unexpected difficulties.

- **Compatibility Issues:** Many firms use antiquated infrastructure that might not be able to handle the implementation of sophisticated AI models.
- **Data Format Incompatibility:** Preprocessing is typically necessary when integrating structured and unstructured data from legacy systems.
- **Real-Time Processing Requirements:** Traditional IT infrastructure may not be able to meet the real-time outputs required by industries such as retail or logistics.

Infrastructure Limitations
- **Scalability Issues:** AI models, particularly expert ones, frequently demand a large amount of processing power, which could impose a burden on the infrastructure that is currently in place.
- **Cloud vs. On-Premises Deployment**: Businesses need to choose between upgrading on-premises hardware for more control and investing in cloud solutions for scalability.
- **Latency and Downtime:** Without careful

infrastructure planning, it might be difficult to guarantee constant model performance under heavy workloads.

Model Upkeep and Updates

To be current and correct, expert models need to be updated on a regular basis:

- Dynamic data integration is the process of modifying models to include fresh data sources without having to start over from scratch.
- **Debugging and Monitoring:** Consistently assessing model performance to detect and address problems such as concept drift.
- **Compliance Updates:** Modifying models to conform to changing regulatory standards.

6.3 Developmental Skill and Cost Gaps

Expert model development is a resource-intensive process that calls for both specialized expertise and monetary investments.

Financial Investments

- **High Development Costs:** Major expenditures in data collection, computing power, and development time are necessary for the creation and training of expert models.

- **Deployment Expenses:** The integration and maintenance of AI models into operational systems may result in continuous expenses.

- **Uncertain ROI Risk:** Without precise ROI estimates, businesses would be hesitant to make significant investments in AI.

Skill Gaps in Development

- **Specialized experience:** Expert model development necessitates a blend of domain-specific knowledge and artificial intelligence experience, which is frequently lacking.

- **Recruitment Challenges:** It might be difficult and competitive to find experts with the correct combination of skills.

- The process of upskilling current personnel to close the talent gap can be a slow but effective way to train existing teams.

Methods to Overcome Cost and Skill Issues

- **Partnership with Academic and Research Institutions:** Collaborating with universities can give access to state-of-the-art information and resources.

- **Adopting Pre-Trained Models:** Using pre-trained models speeds up deployment and lowers costs.

- **Workforce Development Investing:** Provide training courses to current staff members.

- Establish apprenticeships and internships to build a pool of qualified workers.

- **Using AI-as-a-Service Platforms**: Cloud-based AI solutions give businesses access to advanced AI capabilities without having to pay a large sum of money up front.

The process of creating and implementing expert AI models is difficult, but every setback offers a chance for development and innovation. When addressing data challenges, privacy, quality, and fairness must be prioritized. While financial and skill restrictions necessitate innovative solutions like partnerships and pre-trained models, technical integration demands careful preparation and flexibility. Businesses that aggressively address these issues will be in a better position to realize expert AI's transformational potential and succeed in the long run.

CHAPTER 7

ASSESSING AND TRACKING EXPERT MODEL PERFORMANCE

Designing, implementing, and deploying expert models successfully requires a methodical evaluation of their performance. Evaluation aids in making sure that these models are meeting expectations and providing benefits to the company. Measuring success is more complicated than just examining prediction accuracy, though. It takes a thorough approach that includes setting up systems for constant monitoring, creating key performance indicators (KPIs), and using feedback mechanisms to promote continuous improvements. In order to make sure expert models fulfill corporate goals and adjust to changing conditions, this chapter examines how to assess their efficacy.

7.1 Specifying AI Model Success Metrics

The first step in assessing expert models is to establish

precise success indicators. These metrics give firms an objective way to assess how well AI is performing as intended. Some fundamental rules can be applied across many industries, although key performance indicators (KPIs) can vary based on the industry, model aims, and data type.

KPIs, or key performance indicators

KPIs are quantifiable figures that show how well the AI model fits into the objectives of the company. The key performance indicators for assessing expert models are listed below:

Accuracy and Precision: Accuracy is the proportion of accurate predictions among all of the model's predictions. When the ramifications of false positives are substantial, accuracy is essential. For example, the ability of a diagnostic model to accurately detect illnesses without misdiagnosing patients is crucial in the healthcare industry.

The following is the formula for accuracy:

- Accuracy = True Positives + True Negative / Total Predictions

The following is the formula for Precision:

- Precision = True Positives / True Positives + True Negatives

F1-Score and Recall:

Recall, sometimes referred to as sensitivity, quantifies the proportion of real positive examples that the model accurately detected. The F1-Score balances precision and recall by taking the harmonic mean of the two. A high recall value guarantees that the model detects as many real cases as feasible in crucial systems like fraud detection or medical diagnostics.

The formula for recall is as follows:

- Recall = True Positives / True Positives + False Negatives

The F1-Score formula is as follows:

- F1-Score = 2 (Precision * Recall / Precision + Recall)

Beyond conventional measurements like accuracy, it is crucial to match KPIs with the organization's overarching business objectives. This is known as "business-centric KPIs." For instance:

- **ROI (Return on Investment)**: Calculating the amount of profit or savings that the AI model generates relative to the costs of development and operation.

- **Operational Efficiency:** Evaluating enhancements to corporate procedures, including less time spent on operational or decision-making activities. AI models can enhance route optimization in sectors like supply chain management, cutting expenses and delivery times.

- Metrics like Net Promoter Score (NPS) or customer feedback are used to measure how successfully AI models are improving user experiences.

Comparative Benchmarks

When evaluating an expert model's performance against industry norms or rival models, benchmarking is essential. Typical benchmarking techniques include the following:

- The accuracy of human radiologists is one example of an industry-specific benchmark that is frequently used to compare AI models used for medical imaging in the healthcare sector.

- The process of evaluating the performance of various models (such as machine learning versus deep learning) in order to determine which one is most appropriate for the given job is known as "cross-model comparison."

- **Historical Benchmarks:** Assessing advancement or regression by contrasting the performance of the current model with that of earlier models.

7.2 Expert Model Maintenance and Monitoring

In order to stay accurate and relevant over time, AI models, especially expert models, need to be continuously monitored and maintained.

The Significance of Continuous Monitoring

- **Model Drift:** Concept drift is a phenomenon in which the underlying patterns in the data shift with time, impairing the accuracy of the model's predictions. This is especially common in fields like finance and e-commerce that are undergoing rapid change.

- **Changes to the Data:** The model's performance may be affected if the data it was first trained on changes. For example, a model may need to adjust to new trends if customer tastes or market conditions change.

- **Regulatory and Compliance Requirements**: Changing regulations apply to industries like insurance, healthcare, and banking. To be compliant, models need to be updated frequently.

Optimal Monitoring Techniques

- **Real-Time Performance Tracking:** By putting in place mechanisms that continuously check the model's output, performance decline can be promptly detected. When the model's performance falls below a predetermined level, stakeholders can be notified using tools such as anomaly detection systems or model dashboards.

- **Error Analysis:** Monitoring situations in which the model performs badly or fails, and identifying possible data problems or weaknesses in model assumptions by doing root-cause studies.

- **Performance Over Time:** To monitor the model's

capacity to adjust and retain accuracy, continuously assess its performance in relation to the original benchmarks.

Updates and Model Retraining

- **Retraining Frequency:** The industry and the rate of data change determine how often the model needs to be retrained. While more stable sectors could function with fewer upgrades, high-velocity industries like e-commerce may require retraining every few weeks.

- **Learning Incrementally:** The model may continually learn from fresh data without requiring retraining by utilizing online learning or incremental learning techniques.

- **Control of Version:** By keeping version control for every model version, it is possible to compare older and newer versions, revealing both areas of improvement and areas for concern.

7.3 Feedback Loops for Ongoing Improvement

For expert models to continuously improve, feedback

systems are essential. By gaining knowledge from user interactions and system-generated insights, these loops aid in improving model performance.

What Are Loops of Feedback?

The act of evaluating model outputs or predictions and using the results to retrain the model or improve its algorithms is known as a feedback loop. These may be external (user-provided feedback) or internal (data generated by the system).

Feedback Loop Types

- **User Feedback:** End users can offer insightful opinions on how well the model performs. For instance, user preferences or interactions (such as likes, purchases, or viewing history) are continuously used to increase recommendation accuracy in recommendation systems (such as those used by Netflix or Amazon).
- **System Comment:** Feedback based on operational bottlenecks, mistake rates, or the time it takes for a model to analyze fresh data are examples of this. These metrics are essential for enhancing expert

models' robustness, speed, and efficiency.

- **Outside Comments:** External input from regulatory agencies or compliance audits can aid in improving the model's procedures in specific industries. In the financial industry, for example, models can have to adjust to recently implemented compliance rules, necessitating outside input to continue functioning.

Building automated systems that gather data from user interactions in real-time and feed it straight into the model training pipeline is the first step in implementing feedback mechanisms.

- In order to learn and adapt more precisely, the model asks users for input on ambiguous predictions. This process is known as "active learning."

- **Periodic Assessment and Modification:** Experts should examine models on a regular basis to make sure they are operating in line with changing business objectives. For example, when new goods or services are offered, a marketing model that is utilized for consumer segmentation may need to be modified.

Iteration Cycles: Using feedback to create a cycle of ongoing improvement, in which the model's features, parameters, and algorithms are modified iteratively to enhance performance is how Driving Iterative Improvement is accomplished.

- The ability of the model to exceed its prior iterations based on important measures (such as improved accuracy or customer happiness) is how success is judged.
- Involving end users, domain experts, and other stakeholders in the feedback process guarantees that the enhancements are in line with expectations and needs in the real world.

Expert model evaluation and measurement are continuous processes that need systematic feedback integration, constant monitoring, and close attention to important performance indicators. Organizations can evaluate how well their models satisfy business objectives by establishing precise success indicators. Long-term success is fostered by continuous feedback loops that promote incremental improvements and regular monitoring and updates that guarantee models stay relevant in dynamic situations. By mastering this approach, organizations may fully utilize their expert models, guaranteeing that they provide long-term worth and consistently adjust to evolving company requirements.

CHAPTER 8

EXPERT MODELS' FUTURE

Expert models are developing at a quick pace thanks to new and innovative technologies that are constantly changing how AI systems support and interact with human expertise. The integration of new technologies and the convergence of AI models with generative capabilities offer exciting new possibilities as companies depend more and more on AI to solve complicated challenges. The future of expert models is examined in this chapter, with particular attention paid to the technologies that are transforming them, the possible effects of incorporating generative AI, and futuristic scenarios of how various industries can change as a result of the broad use of these cutting-edge models.

8.1 Expert Models Shaped by Emerging Technologies

With new technologies emerging that promise to improve

their capabilities, scalability, and adaptability, the expert model environment is changing dramatically. The construction, implementation, and operation of these models are being redefined by significant advancements like edge computing, federated learning, and quantum AI. In addition to altering expert models' performance, these technologies are broadening the range of capabilities that these models may accomplish.

Decentralizing AI Processing: Edge Computing

Processing data closer to its source rather than depending entirely on centralized cloud-based systems is known as edge computing. AI models can analyze data more quickly and with less bandwidth usage by locating computing resources at the network's edge, such as on local servers or Internet of Things devices.

- **Decreased Latency:** The decrease in latency is one of the main advantages of edge computing for expert models. Instant feedback is essential for real-time applications like heath monitoring or driverless cars. Expert models can make judgments more quickly because of edge computing, which eliminates the need for data to travel to and from remote cloud servers.

- **Enhanced Security and Privacy:** Edge computing contributes to the protection of user privacy by storing private information locally. In sectors like healthcare and finance, where adherence to laws like HIPAA and GDPR is crucial, this is especially crucial. Data may be processed securely with edge computing, protecting it from possible security breaches.

- **Scalability:** Edge computing makes it possible to scale AI models without overburdening centralized data centers as the number of IoT devices rises. In sectors like manufacturing, where real-time data processing may support operational optimization and predictive maintenance, this scalability creates new opportunities.

Collaborative Model Training: Federated Learning

A distributed machine learning method called federated learning enables several devices or organizations to work together to build an AI model without exchanging raw data. Rather, the model is trained on local data by each participant, and only model updates are shared, which are then combined centrally.

- **Privacy and Security of Data:** Because data never leaves the local device or server, federated learning improves privacy. For industries where data sensitivity is crucial, like healthcare and finance, this is especially advantageous. Without disclosing specific data points, the model may nevertheless learn from a big dataset.

- **Inter-Institution Cooperation:** Federated learning allows several hospitals, research institutes, or pharmaceutical corporations to work together on training AI models for medical diagnosis or drug discovery in sectors like healthcare. Expert model creation is accelerated by this cooperative method without sacrificing data privacy.

- **Effectiveness and Adaptability:** Federated learning reduces the bandwidth and storage needs while enabling models to be trained on a variety of datasets from several sources. This is especially helpful for enterprises with limited access to centralized data infrastructure or in remote locations.

Unlocking New Computational Power: Quantum AI

The fast developing discipline of quantum computing uses the laws of quantum mechanics to carry out calculations that are either impossible or extremely inefficient when done by traditional computers. Even while quantum AI is still in its infancy, its unparalleled processing capacity has the potential to completely transform expert models.

- **Optimized Performance:** AI models may be able to carry out optimization tasks like model search and hyperparameter tuning more effectively thanks to quantum computers. Expert models in sectors like banking, healthcare, and logistics may become quicker and more accurate as a result.

- **Resolving Complicated Issues:** Quantum algorithms could be used to solve a number of issues that are now unsolvable by classical computers, such as optimizing large-scale supply chains or simulating chemical interactions in drug discovery. By allowing expert models to evaluate enormous volumes of data and produce incredibly accurate predictions, quantum AI may result in advances in several domains.

- **Efficiency and Speed:** Simulation and data processing times could be significantly shortened by quantum AI models. Expert models will be able to be scaled up for real-time applications like robotics, tailored medicine, and driverless cars because of its efficiency.

8.2 The Combination of Generative AI and Expert Models

One of the most interesting developments in artificial intelligence is generative AI, which produces new information by using patterns discovered in current data. New possibilities for creativity, innovation, and problem-solving are made possible by the combination of generative AI with expert models. Organizations may accomplish previously unthinkable results by fusing the creativity and adaptability of generative AI with the skills of expert models, which are excellent at making decisions and solving problems within a certain domain.

Opening Up New Horizons for Innovation

Conventionally inflexible expert systems can be made more creative with generative AI. With a thorough understanding of chemical structures and biological processes, generative AI could assist in the design of completely new therapeutic compounds in sectors like pharmaceuticals. Faster drug research and discovery can arise from the validation of these generative findings by expert models trained on medical data.

- **The discovery of drugs:** Novel molecular structures that would not be immediately apparent to human researchers could be produced by generative models, such as those built on variational autoencoders (VAEs) or generative adversarial networks (GANs). The drug development pipeline can be expedited by using expert models that have been trained on medical data to assess these produced compounds for possible efficacy and safety.

- **Design and Production:** Generative AI has the potential to produce innovative product designs, architectures, or solutions in the design and manufacturing industries. These designs can subsequently be evaluated by expert models according to criteria including material restrictions, cost-effectiveness, and manufacturability. Innovations in fields ranging from consumer goods to aerospace engineering may result from this mutually beneficial link between generative AI and expert models.

- **Creativity and Art**: Literature, music, and art are already being produced with generative AI. The creative output can be improved, customized, and adapted to particular user preferences by including expert models into this process. For instance, an expert model trained on user data may tailor the composition to the listener's preferences, while a generative AI model could compose a piece of music.

Customized Encounters

- Generative AI can be used to produce tailored content or recommendations in consumer-facing sectors like retail and entertainment. By comprehending user preferences and tailoring the generating output to individual preferences, expert models can improve this customisation.

- **Generating Content:** Customers can receive personalized content from generative AI in the form of interactive experiences, ads, or suggestions. By ensuring that these recommendations are in line with consumer trends and preferences, expert models can raise customer engagement and satisfaction.

- **Products that can be customized:** Generative AI can produce product designs that are configurable in sectors like fashion, enabling buyers to customize their purchases. In addition to forecasting demand for specific customizations, expert models can guarantee that these designs are scalable and satisfy quality requirements.

8.3 Expert Model Scenarios for 2030 and Later

Expert models will keep developing and be essential to the transformation of industries in 2030 and beyond. Expert models will influence how companies run, how services are provided, and how individuals use technology as AI becomes more ingrained in our daily lives and work routines.

Medicine: Tailored, Instantaneous Diagnosis and Therapy

Expert models that offer highly individualized, real-time diagnosis and treatment suggestions have the potential to revolutionize healthcare by 2030. Expert models will be able to examine genetic, environmental, and lifestyle data to develop customized treatment regimens for individuals as a result of developments in AI, genomics, and personalized medicine.

- **AI-Powered Precision Healthcare:** In order to create individualized treatment regimens, AI models will be able to evaluate enormous volumes of health data from wearables, genomic sequencing, and electronic medical records. To suggest the best course of action, these expert models will take into account each patient's particular medical history, genetic composition, and lifestyle choices.

- **Health Monitoring in Real Time:** Through linked gadgets, expert models will continuously monitor patients' health, offering real-time insights into illnesses like mental health disorders or chronic diseases. This will lower hospital visits and enhance overall healthcare outcomes by enabling prompt intervention when needed.

Finance: Fraud Prevention and Autonomous Financial Systems

Expert models in finance will automate a number of financial management tasks, such as fraud detection, risk assessment, and investment decision-making. AI-powered systems will be able to decide on investments on their own by 2030, using current market conditions and data.

- **Risk Management with Predictive Analytics:** To

forecast financial risks and suggest mitigation techniques, expert models will make use of huge datasets, such as macroeconomic and market movements. Credit rating, insurance underwriting, and portfolio management will all heavily rely on these models.

- The prevention and detection of fraud: In order to identify fraud and stop financial crimes, AI models will continuously track financial transactions in real time. Expert models will be able to detect fraudulent activity before it does serious harm by examining past transaction data and seeing odd trends.

Autonomous Systems: Robotics and Intelligent Vehicles
Expert models that allow autonomous systems to make complicated judgments in real-time will determine the future of autonomous systems, from robots to self-driving cars. Expert models will be essential to the functioning of autonomous robots and intelligent cars by 2030, guaranteeing their efficiency, safety, and adaptability in changing conditions.

- **Autonomous Automobiles:** Vehicles will be able to make decisions about navigation, obstacle avoidance, and route optimization in real time thanks to expert models. By continuously learning from sensor data, these models will enhance the car's capacity to drive safely in varying traffic situations.

- The use of robotics in manufacturing As robotics advances, robots will be guided by expert models in jobs like maintenance, assembly, and quality assurance. These systems will be extremely versatile and effective since they can adjust to different tasks and settings.

Expert models have a bright future ahead of them. Expert models will grow more potent, flexible, and essential to corporate operations as cutting-edge technologies like edge computing, federated learning, and quantum AI expand the realm of what is possible. The combination of generative AI and expert models will enable unprecedented levels of personalization, creativity, and innovation. Expert models will play a key role in the drastic transformation of sectors like healthcare, banking, and transportation by 2030.

crucial part in determining how technology develops in the future.

CHAPTER 9

REGULATORY AND ETHICAL ASPECTS

In order to ensure that artificial intelligence (AI) technologies are created, implemented, and used ethically, ethical and regulatory issues are crucial as AI continues to advance and becomes a crucial component of decision-making across industries. This is especially true for expert models, which can impact financial systems, healthcare results, corporate strategies, and more. To make sure that these models are not only successful but also in line with social values, it is crucial to address issues like justice, openness, and trust in addition to navigating the complicated regulatory environment. In order to overcome prejudice, maintain fairness, and assure openness while adhering to industry standards and promoting user trust, this chapter explores the ethical and regulatory issues underlying expert models.

9.1 Making Sure Expert Models Are Fair and Open

Ensuring justice and transparency is one of the main ethical issues facing AI. From diagnosing medical issues to granting loans, expert models are frequently employed to make critical choices. Since these choices have a big influence on people's lives, it is crucial to make sure the models are impartial, open, and equitable.

Tackling Expert Model Bias

Biased data, biased algorithms, or biased assumptions made during model creation are some of the origins of bias in AI models. Bias has the potential to provide unjust results, maintain current disparities, and erode public confidence in AI systems.

- **Recognizing Bias in Data:** Finding bias in the data is the first step towards correcting it. Because AI models are only as good as the data they are trained on, they will reinforce prejudices if the data contains historical biases or biased representation. For instance, a recruiting algorithm may unjustly disfavor female applicants if the dataset used to train it has a large number of male applications. Organizations must make sure that the data used to train expert models is balanced, representative, and devoid of discriminating trends in order to reduce this risk.

- **Fairness-Conscious Algorithms:** Fairness-aware algorithms can be incorporated by developers to address biases during the model-building phase. These algorithms are made to take into consideration things like treatment equality, equality of opportunity, and demographic parity. Even when working with faulty data, businesses can lower the danger of biased conclusions by integrating fairness into the algorithm itself.

- **Continuous Model Auditing:** Detecting bias should be a continuous process rather than a one-time event. To make sure that expert models continue to function impartially over time, external and internal auditors must conduct routine audits for fairness. This involves assessing models after they are deployed in order to find and fix any potential inadvertent discrimination.

Preserving Openness in Expert Models

To make sure that stakeholders are aware of the decision-making process, transparency in AI is essential. Because expert models frequently function as "black boxes," it can be challenging for users to comprehend the logic underlying their predictions. This lack of openness can erode confidence and cause accountability issues.

- **Decision-Making Explainability:** The creation of explainable AI (XAI) is one strategy for improving transparency. XAI approaches seek to improve the interpretability of complicated models by offering human-comprehensible justifications for their choices. A medical expert model that suggests a certain course of therapy, for example, would benefit from an explanation that focuses on the important elements (such as the patient's medical history and the findings of diagnostic tests) that shaped the decision.

- The process of model auditing Organizations should use comprehensive model auditing procedures in addition to XAI to monitor the decision-making process. This could entail keeping thorough logs that document the features the model uses and the logic underlying its predictions. When concerns are raised over the accuracy or fairness of the model's judgments, these logs may be extremely important.

- **Openness in the Use of Data:** The sources, processing methods, and any biases of the data used to train expert models should all be openly disclosed by organizations. Giving consumers comprehensive documentation on data sources and gathering techniques can help to achieve this transparency. Organizations can improve the reliability of their models by increasing the transparency of the data pipeline.

Assuring Accountability and Fairness

To guarantee that expert models do not disproportionately

hurt any group, fairness and accountability must be given top priority. This calls for a multifaceted strategy that incorporates accountability frameworks, model testing, and bias identification.

- **Partnership with Stakeholders:** Involving a wide variety of stakeholders in the development process is crucial to achieving fairness. Data scientists, subject matter specialists, ethicists, and members of impacted communities are all included in this. Organizations can guarantee that expert models are just and equal for all groups by taking into account a variety of viewpoints.

- **Methods of Accountability:** Expert models can be utilized responsibly by putting accountability measures in place, such as effect assessments and fairness benchmarks. Financial firms that use expert models for credit scoring, for instance, must carry out impact analyses to determine whether the model unfairly disadvantages any particular demographic. Organizations will also be held more responsible for their AI systems if model decision-making is transparent and explicit processes are established for contesting unfair choices.

9.2 Managing Industry Standards and Regulations

Governments and regulatory agencies are creating rules and regulations to control the use of AI as it becomes more prevalent in daily life. Navigating the complicated regulatory environment is crucial for businesses creating and implementing expert models in order to maintain compliance and minimize legal risks.

Expert Model Compliance Requirements

The usage of AI and data-driven technology is subject to stringent laws in a number of industries, including finance, healthcare, and education. For instance, financial institutions are required to abide by laws that forbid discrimination in lending practices, such as the Fair Lending Act and the Equal Credit Opportunity Act (ECOA). Likewise, in order to safeguard patient privacy, healthcare practitioners are required to comply with the Health Insurance Portability and Accountability Act

(HIPAA).

- **Privacy and Protection of Data:** Data privacy is one of the most important regulatory issues in the creation of expert models. Companies now have to make sure that personal data is managed carefully and that people's right to privacy is upheld in light of laws like California's Consumer Privacy Act (CCPA) and the European Union's General Data Protection Regulation (GDPR). To utilize people's data, organizations need to get their express consent and be open and honest about how they plan to use it.

- **Model Documentation and Audits:** Documenting the creation and use of AI models is a requirement in most regulatory systems. This entails keeping track of the information used, the algorithms applied, and the choices the model made. To make sure the company conforms with industry standards, auditors or regulators should have easy access to these documents.

- **Regulations at the Cross-Border Level:** AI

systems are frequently implemented internationally in the modern global economy. When implementing expert models, organizations need to take into account the differing rules in other nations. For example, regardless of an organization's location, GDPR is applicable to all entities that handle the personal data of EU individuals. Therefore, it is crucial for businesses that operate globally to comprehend and abide by cross-border data privacy laws.

New Rules Which Affect Expert Models

Regulators are constantly creating new guidelines and regulations to guarantee the responsible application of AI as its use grows. The proposed Artificial Intelligence Act from the European Union, for instance, aims to categorize AI systems according to their degree of danger and set standards for high-risk applications, such as those involving law enforcement, healthcare, and essential infrastructure.

- **Assessment of AI Risk:** Organizations creating

expert models might have to perform risk assessments to determine the possible harm such systems could create under new restrictions. High-risk AI systems, like those in autonomous driving or healthcare, can be subject to more stringent regulatory scrutiny and need for more thorough documentation, openness, and supervision.

- **Guides for Ethical AI:** To ensure the proper use of AI, numerous governments and regulatory agencies are now establishing ethical AI guidelines. Fairness, accountability, and openness in AI systems are the goals of these standards. To guarantee compliance, companies that create expert models should keep up with these recommendations and apply them to their development procedures.

9.3 Establishing Credibility with AI Systems

The acceptance of AI is based on trust. Users must think that the system is trustworthy, equitable, and transparent in order for them to completely accept expert models. It takes a concentrated effort to prioritize explainability, guarantee accountability, and adhere to responsible AI policies in order to develop trust in AI systems.

The Function of Explainability in Establishing Credibility

For expert models to be trusted, explainability is essential. Users are more inclined to trust a system when they know how it makes its decisions. For instance, in the medical field, both physicians and patients must comprehend the logic underlying AI-driven diagnosis and therapy suggestions. Giving concise, intelligible justifications for a model's reasoning behind a given conclusion helps boost trust in the model's fairness and accuracy.

- **The interactive explanations are as follows:** By providing interactive explanations that let users examine the logic underlying model decisions, organizations can improve explainability. A user interface that enables a financial adviser to click on particular elements that affect a credit score prediction, for instance, can promote a greater level of comprehension and confidence in the system.

- **Systems with Humans in the Loop:**
  Human-in-the-loop (HITL) systems, in which human
  specialists examine and verify AI-driven judgments,
  are advantageous for certain AI applications. While
  giving users the assurance that the system is not
  acting alone, this hybrid method can guarantee that
  AI recommendations are in line with human ethics
  and values.

Conscious AI Methods

Respecting ethical AI practices is another way to foster
trust. This involves making certain that ethical issues are
taken into account while developing AI systems and that
their application is consistent with society norms.

- **Openness in Development:** Establishing trust
  requires open and honest growth procedures. The
  entire process of developing an expert model, from
  gathering data to training and deploying the model,
  should be explained in detail by organizations.
  Setting reasonable expectations can also be

facilitated by being forthright about the difficulties and constraints of AI systems.

- **Constant Observation and Enhancement:** Transparency at the beginning of a project is not the only way to establish trust. It also necessitates ongoing observation and development. To preserve confidence, organizations must evaluate the effectiveness of their expert models on a regular basis, handle any new ethical issues that arise, and upgrade the system as needed.

- The concept of accountability In the end, accountability determines whether or not AI systems can be trusted. Organizations must accept responsibility for the outcome and take corrective action if an expert model makes a mistake or yields unjust results. Users can hold companies responsible for the choices made by AI systems if explicit accountability frameworks are established.

The proper creation and application of expert models depends heavily on ethical and regulatory issues. To make sure AI systems are deployed in a way that benefits all stakeholders, it is crucial to address fairness, ensure transparency, navigate industry rules, and cultivate trust. Organizations can create expert models that fulfill commercial goals and advance society by following these guidelines.

CHAPTER 10

EXPERT MODEL ADOPTION STRATEGIES FOR ORGANIZATIONS

An organized and systematic strategy is required when businesses investigate the use of expert models to enhance decision-making and optimize operations. By automating difficult decisions and boosting productivity, expert models can revolutionize organizational processes in a variety of industries, including marketing, finance, healthcare, and others. Nevertheless, incorporating such models necessitates meticulous preparation, assessment, and cooperation. From evaluating preparedness to creating a thorough roadmap and working with outside partners, this chapter offers a thorough examination of the actions that businesses should take in order to successfully use expert models.

10.1 Evaluating AI Implementation Readiness

Organizations must evaluate their preparedness before

starting the expert model implementation process. This assessment shows that the company has the infrastructure, culture, and resources needed to facilitate the deployment of AI. Before proceeding, a readiness assessment framework offers a path for resolving these issues and assists enterprises in identifying gaps in their AI capabilities.

1. Mindset and Organizational Culture

Implementing expert models necessitates a change in company culture in addition to technology. Adoption of AI should not be seen as a threat to the existing quo, but rather as a chance for advancement. A culture that values data-driven decision-making and acknowledges the significance of AI technology must be promoted by the leadership.

- **Support for Leadership:** Adoption of AI requires strong leadership commitment. In order to align the entire organization with the vision of AI deployment, leaders should facilitate cross-functional collaboration, allocate resources, and promote AI initiatives.

- **Input from Employees**: Adoption of AI should be explained in detail to staff members at all levels. Addressing worries, clearing up myths around job displacement, and highlighting how AI may enhance human capabilities rather than replace them are all vital.

2. Quality and Data Infrastructure

The effectiveness of expert models is largely dependent on the quality of the data. To gather, store, and process high-quality data, organizations need to evaluate if they have the required data architecture in place.

- **Availability of Data:** Large amounts of high-quality data are necessary for expert models. Businesses should determine if they have the data needed to properly train these models. For example, in order to create credit scoring models, banking companies need precise transaction histories, and healthcare providers need thorough patient data.

- **Data Integrity and Quality**: AI models rely on precise, comprehensive, and consistent data. To guarantee data quality, organizations need to put strong data governance procedures into place. This covers data validation, data cleansing, and making sure the data is free of biases that can influence model results.

3. Infrastructure and Technical Capabilities

To make sure the company has the resources and infrastructure needed to create and use expert models successfully, it is essential to evaluate technical preparedness.

- **Stack of Technology:** The expectations of AI models must be met by the organization's technology stack. This entails having the software frameworks (like TensorFlow, PyTorch, or other machine learning platforms), processing power, and storage options required to create, train, and implement expert models.

97

- **Talent Pool:** An organization's internal technical skills need to be evaluated. Do they have the AI experts, machine learning engineers, and data scientists they need? If not, are they prepared to make the investment to hire new talent or upskill their current staff in order to cover these gaps?

4. Compliance with Law, Ethics, and Regulations

Businesses need to make sure that their AI models abide by all applicable laws and moral standards. This entails being aware of the legal frameworks governing model openness, bias mitigation, and data privacy.

- **Compliance with Regulations**: To make sure they can gather and use data for AI models in a way that complies with the law, organizations should evaluate their current compliance with regulations such as the General Data Protection Regulation (GDPR), the California Consumer Privacy Act (CCPA), and the Health Insurance Portability and Accountability Act (HIPAA).

- **Guidelines for Ethics:** Organizations should set ethical standards for the creation and application of AI models in addition to regulatory compliance. Fairness, accountability, and openness in AI decision-making are a few examples of this.

5. Resource Allocation and Budget

Lastly, using expert models necessitates a large financial outlay. Businesses should evaluate their financial preparedness to pay for the expenses associated with using AI, such as recruiting personnel, making infrastructural investments, acquiring AI solutions, and continuing maintenance.

- **Cost Evaluation:** Organizations may comprehend the return on investment (ROI) of implementing expert models by doing a comprehensive cost-benefit analysis. For example, businesses might have to weigh the upfront setup expenses against the long-term operational savings and efficiencies from implementing AI.

10.2 Creating an AI Roadmap: From Idea to Implementation

Creating a thorough AI plan is the next step once an organization has evaluated its preparedness. The strategic actions required to proceed from the development of expert models to their implementation and expansion inside the company are delineated in this roadmap. AI initiatives stay on course and in line with corporate objectives when they have a clear roadmap.

1. Outlining Specific Goals and Use Cases

Establishing precise goals and determining the organization's expert model use cases is the first stage in creating an AI roadmap. This entails being aware of the issues AI is intended to address and how it fits in with corporate objectives.

- **Alignment of Business:** The goals of AI projects ought to be in line with the overarching business plan. For instance, a financial company may use machine learning to increase fraud detection capabilities, while a hospital firm may use predictive analytics to improve patient outcomes.

- **Setting Use Case Priorities:** The use cases that are most valuable and practical to execute should be given priority by companies after the goals have been established. Data availability, task complexity, and anticipated business impact are some of the elements that should be taken into consideration while choosing early use cases.

2. Establishing the Development Team for AI"

Putting together a diverse team capable of completing the project from conception to implementation is essential for a successful AI roadmap.

- **Engineers and data scientists**: To create and train the expert models, a group of knowledgeable data scientists and machine learning engineers is required. They are in charge of choosing features, specifying the model architecture, and making sure the models satisfy performance standards.

- **SMEs, or subject matter experts:** The importance of domain-specific expertise varies by industry. For instance, in order to guarantee that the expert models are safe and clinically relevant, medical practitioners may need to collaborate with AI specialists.

- **Manager of AI Project**: By supervising the development process, an AI project manager may guarantee that the project remains on course, that deadlines are fulfilled, and that resources are distributed efficiently.

3. Choosing and Constructing Appropriate Tools and Technology

Having the appropriate technology and tools in place is essential for the success of expert models. Businesses must choose between using pre-built solutions or developing their own AI models.

- The difference between in-house development and

third-party solutions While some businesses might choose to use third-party AI solutions, others might want to create expert models from the ground up. For instance, businesses can select from a variety of cloud services (including Google Cloud, AWS, and Azure), machine learning platforms, or specific AI tools that could speed up development.

- **Planning for Infrastructure:** AI models demand a large amount of processing power. Businesses must budget for the cloud infrastructure and hardware required for large-scale model deployment and training.

4. Validation, Testing, and Model Training

Organizations must concentrate on model training and validation after the infrastructure and tools are in place. This phase is essential to guaranteeing that the expert models are precise, trustworthy, and in line with corporate objectives.

- **Model Training:** AI experts will train the expert

models to identify trends and forecast outcomes using previous data. The team may test out several algorithms during this stage and adjust the model's parameters for best results.

- **Model Testing and Validation:** To assess the models' performance and make sure they generalize well to new data, they should be validated using different test datasets after training. To evaluate the model's efficacy, important measures like accuracy, precision, recall, and F1 score should be employed.

- **Iterative Enhancements:** The process of creating AI models is iterative. Based on testing input, the team should continuously improve the models and release new iterations over time.

5. Scaling and Deployment

Organizations can proceed with deployment after the models have been trained and verified. This entails scaling the models to accommodate real-time decision-making and incorporating them into current business procedures.

- **Pilot's Implementation**: Before a full-scale deployment, businesses can assess the expert model's performance in a real-world environment with the use of a pilot implementation. This guarantees that the model is in line with corporate goals and permits any necessary modifications.

- **Maintenance and Monitoring:** Following deployment, ongoing observation is required to guarantee the model maintains its accuracy and functionality. Models may eventually need to be retrained in light of fresh data or modifications brought about by shifting business circumstances.

10.3 Working with Partners and AI Vendors

Expert model adoption and success can be accelerated for many enterprises by working with AI suppliers and technology partners. AI vendors may help businesses use AI more quickly and effectively by providing pre-built solutions, cutting-edge tools, and specialized knowledge.

1. Selecting the Proper AI Provider

Organizations should think about things like the vendor's reputation, experience, and capacity to satisfy their unique requirements when choosing an AI supplier.

- **Skills and Experience:** Select suppliers who have a track record of success in the field or industry where the expert model will be used. For example, a financial institution may seek suppliers with experience in fraud detection, while a healthcare provider might seek AI vendors with knowledge of medical data analytics.

- **Support and Customization:** It's critical to evaluate the vendor's ability to adapt solutions to the unique needs of the company. Maintenance services, training, and post-deployment support should also be taken into account.

2. Development through Collaboration

During the development stage, companies might work

together with technology partners and vendors. This can involve sharing resources and expertise, integrating current technologies with the organization's infrastructure, and co-developing unique AI models.

- **Common Knowledge:** By collaborating with an AI vendor, businesses can benefit from outside knowledge in fields like cloud computing, AI ethics, and machine learning model building. This can expedite the development of AI and support internal teams.

- **Joint Validation and Testing:** Working together with vendors on testing and validation guarantees that the expert models are in line with company objectives and fulfill the necessary performance standards.

3. Using Partners to Scale AI

Having trustworthy technology partners is crucial as businesses expand their AI projects. In order to ensure that expert models can manage growing data volumes and complexity, AI suppliers can assist enterprises in extending their AI capabilities.

- **Scalable Solutions:** Technology partners offer infrastructure that is scalable and can expand along with the company. This can include data pipelines that enable the expert models to analyze more datasets, storage options, and cloud computing resources.

- **International Integration and Reach:** AI suppliers can offer the assistance required for market integration to businesses growing internationally, guaranteeing that expert models operate well in various locales and adhere to local laws.

Implementing expert models is a multi-step, intricate procedure that calls for thorough preparation, a well-defined plan, and cooperation with partners and manufacturers of AI. Businesses will be in a better position to successfully integrate expert models and realize the full potential of AI if they take the time to evaluate their readiness, create an AI strategy, and collaborate closely with outside partners.

ABOUT THE AUTHOR

 Author and thought leader in the IT field Taylor Royce is well known. He has a two-decade career and is an expert at tech trend analysis and forecasting, which enables a wide audience to understand complicated concepts.

Royce's considerable involvement in the IT industry stemmed from his passion with technology, which he developed during his computer science studies. He has extensive knowledge of the industry because of his experience in both software development and strategic consulting.

Known for his research and lucidity, he has written multiple best-selling books and contributed to esteemed tech periodicals. Translations of Royce's books throughout the world demonstrate his impact.

Royce is a well-known authority on emerging technologies and their effects on society, frequently requested as a speaker at international conferences and as a guest on tech podcasts. He promotes the development of ethical technology, emphasizing problems like data privacy and the digital divide.

In addition, with a focus on sustainable industry growth, Royce mentors upcoming tech experts and supports IT education projects. Taylor Royce is well known for his ability to combine analytical thinking with technical know-how. He sees a time when technology will ethically benefit humanity.

www.ingramcontent.com/pod-product-compliance
Lightning Source LLC
LaVergne TN
LVHW022351060326
832902LV00022B/4385